PULLOXHILL
LOWER SCHOOL

USING MAPS

Nature's habitats

by Susan Hoe

ticktock

By Susan Hoe
Series consultant: Debra Voege
Editor: Mark Sachner
Project manager: Joe Harris
ticktock designer: Hayley Terry
Picture research: Lizzie Knowles and Joe Harris

Copyright © 2008 ticktock Entertainment Ltd.
First published in Great Britain by ticktock Media Ltd.,
Unit 2, Orchard Business Centre, North Farm Road, Tunbridge Wells, Kent TN2 3XF, Great Britain.

All rights reserved. No part of this publication may be reproduced, stored in a retrieval system, or transmitted in any form or by any means electronic, mechanical, photocopying, recording or otherwise, without prior written permission of the copyright owner.

A CIP catalogue record for this book is available from the British Library.

ISBN 978 1 84696 723 8

Printed in China

PICTURE CREDITS

getmapping PLC: 24tc. Mike Hill/ Alamy: 14b. Imagebroker/ Alamy: 18c, 30b. iStock: 2, 10cr, 13t, 13b, 17c, 17b, 22t, 25b. Jupiter Images: 7b. www.mapart.co.uk: 7t, 12, 14c, 16c, 20c, 22b, 23, 26, 31tr. Ulli Seer/ Getty Images: 5t. Shutterstock: 4bl, 6b, 8, 11, 16b, 17t, 20bl, 20br, 24tl, 24b, 25t, 25c, 27 all. Justin Spain: 4br, 9, 19b. Doug Steley/ Alamy: 19t. Hayley Terry: 5b, 10bl, 21, 28, 29. ticktock Media Archive: 15. TongRo Image Stock/ Fotosearch: 4t. Dave Watts/ Alamy: 18bl, 18br.

Contents

What is a map? 4

Why do we need maps? 6

Mapping a garden 8

Mapping habitats in a town 10

Mapping habitats in my country 12

Mapping world habitats 14

A map of habitats in Australia 16

Mapping a watering hole in Australia 18

More map information 20

Drawing maps 22

Hi-tech mapmaking 24

Using a grid to map animal habitats in Australia 26

Making a map of a habitat zoo 28

Glossary 30

Index 32

Words in **bold** are explained in the glossary.

What is a map?

A map is a special drawing. This drawing is usually of an area as seen from above.

This area can be as big as the world. Or it can be as small as a single garden!

Making a map of an island

Map Key

- Trees/woods
- Roads/footpaths
- Grey-roofed buildings
- Red-roofed buildings
- Pier
- Gardens

Maps help us find things as if we were directly above them.

In this book, we will see how maps show us about natural **habitats**. These are places where animals and plants make their homes.

Find a wood in the photo of the island.

Now find it on the map.

Why do we need maps?

Maps help us find our way around. They give us all kinds of information about where we live!

A map can help you get from one place to another. It can show you where you are, where you want to go, and how to get there.

Weather map of the UK and Ireland

This map shows you what the weather will be like where you live.

Can you tell what kind of weather this map is showing?

World map

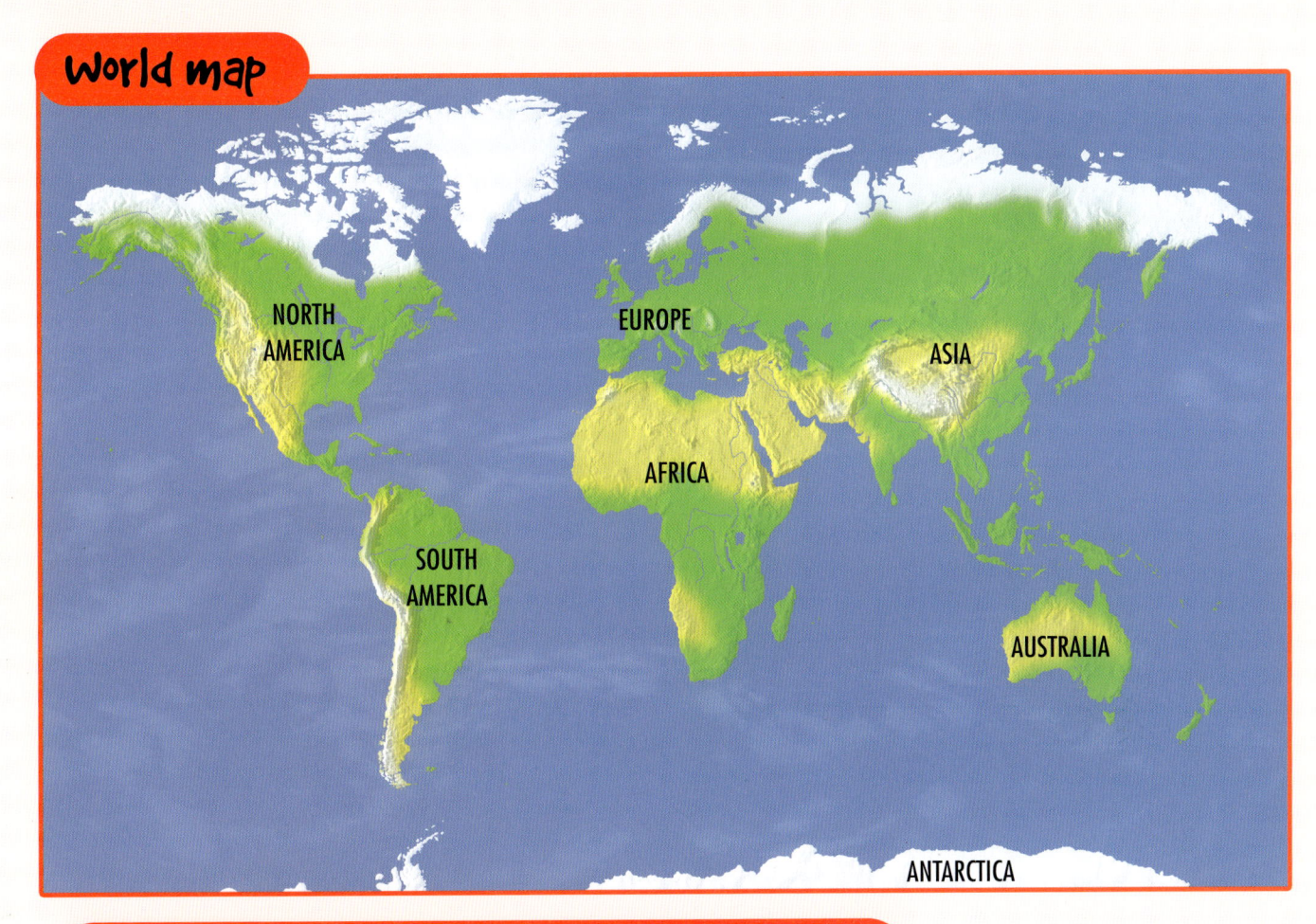

This map shows the world's deserts in yellow. The forests and woods are in green. Places covered in snow and ice are white.

Maps teach us important facts about places. These places might be close to home or far away. Maps show us whether the land is flat or hilly.

They can show what crops are grown and what kinds of things are made in certain places. Maps can show what kinds of animals live in different places.

Maps are handy and easy to use. They can show us huge areas in a small amount of space. We can take them just about anywhere!

Mapping a garden

Maps look down on a place from above. That place can be a country or a town. It can even be a garden! A garden is a habitat where animals, plants, and other things live.

A 3-D garden

This garden is a **three-dimensional** (**3-D**) space. All of the things in it are solid. They have length, width, and **depth**.

A 2-D map

A map is a flat, or **two dimensional (2-D)**, drawing of a space. In a map, all of the objects in the garden look flat. They have only length and width.

To create the 2-D map, we draw all the flat shapes on a piece of paper.

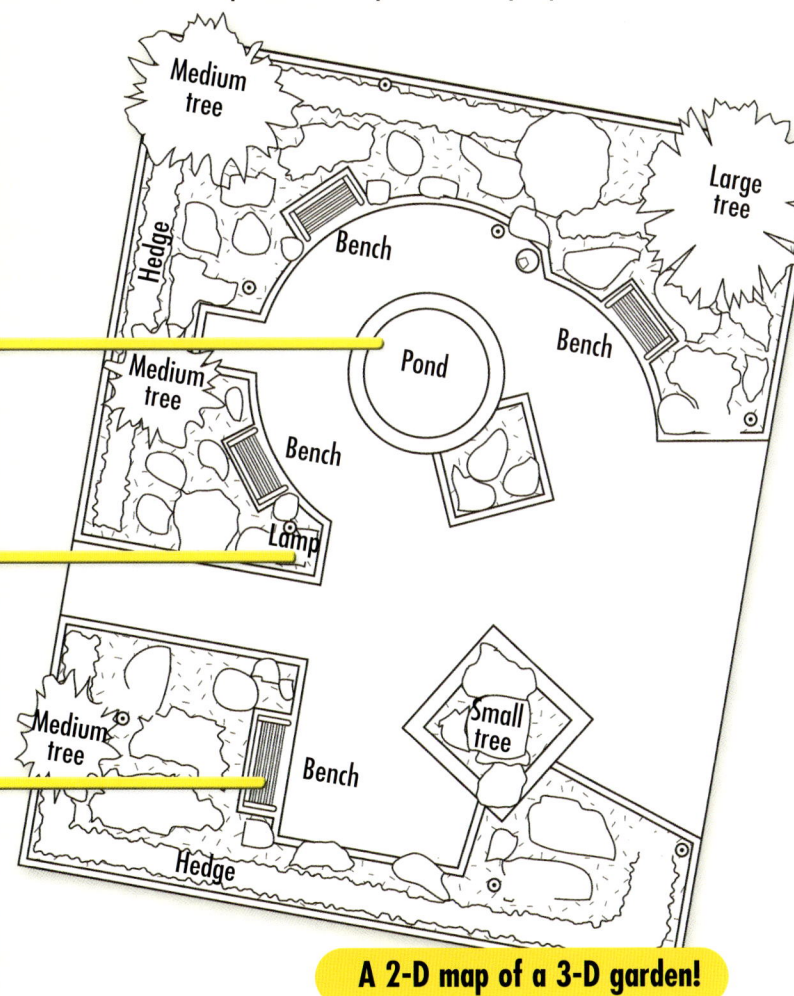

A 2-D map of a 3-D garden!

This map shows you how to find everything in the garden.

Can you find a habitat in this garden where a frog could live?

Making the map

This drawing of the garden was made from the photograph.

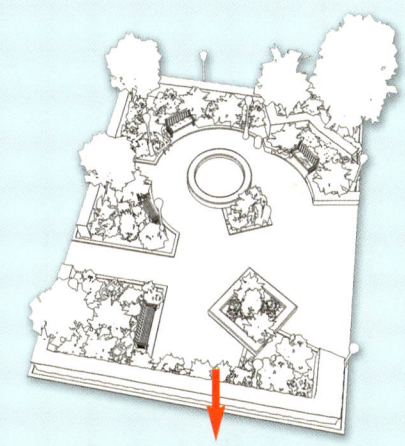

Pretend you are able to float above the garden and look down on it.

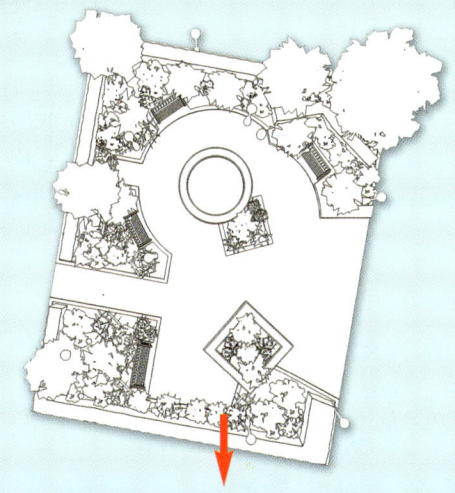

To create the 2-D map, draw all of the garden shapes that you see from above on a piece of paper. Make them flat shapes.

Mapping habitats in a town

Habitats are everywhere. Try to spot different habitats around your town.

Map Key
- Houses
- Large trees
- Small trees
- Woodland
- Lakes
- Fields

The map on the left shows some of the habitats found in this town (above). It uses different **symbols** to identify each place. The map has a key. This **map key** is also called a legend. It tells you what each symbol means.

Can you name three different habitats in the town?

Ecosystems

Many animals live in a habitat with plants and microbes. Microbes are tiny living things so small you can't even see them.

Together, plants, animals and microbes form a community called an ecosystem. They rely on each other to live.

This drawing shows a simple ecosystem in a woodland habitat. If there is a change to any one part, the other parts can be affected.

The bird eats insects and fallen tree seeds.

The bird drops the seeds.

More trees grow from the seeds.

The trees drop their leaves.

Microbes break down the leaves and make them rot.

Insects eat the rotted leaves.

Mapping habitats in my country

There are many different habitats in the United Kingdom. Each has its own kind of land and weather. Each has its own plants and animals.

Look at some of the habitats found on this map of the United Kingdom. Use the map key to see the type of habitat in each area.

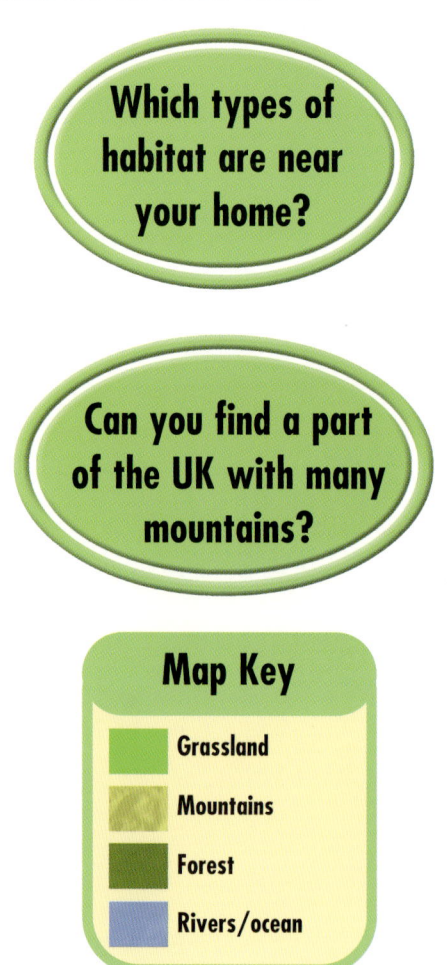

Which types of habitat are near your home?

Can you find a part of the UK with many mountains?

Map Key
- Grassland
- Mountains
- Forest
- Rivers/ocean

Wilderness habitats

Some habitats are found in city or town parks. One such habitat might be a river or a stream. Even the soil beneath a rock can be a habitat for all kinds of plant and insect life! Other habitats contain even more kinds of wildlife. Many of these **wilderness** habitats are protected areas. The **government** makes sure that people do not harm plants and animals living in these areas.

The Cairngorms is a national park in Scotland. There are many habitats here: mountains, valleys, rivers, forests, lakes, and **moorland**. The highest mountain peaks have no trees, but they support mosses and hardy mountain plants.

The red deer (right) and the roe deer roam through the forests of the Cairngorms.

Mapping world habitats

Maps of the world show that Earth has large areas of land called continents. There are seven continents in the world: Europe, Africa, North America, South America, Asia, Australia and Antarctica. You can find many habitats on each of them. There are also habitats in the open waters around the continents.

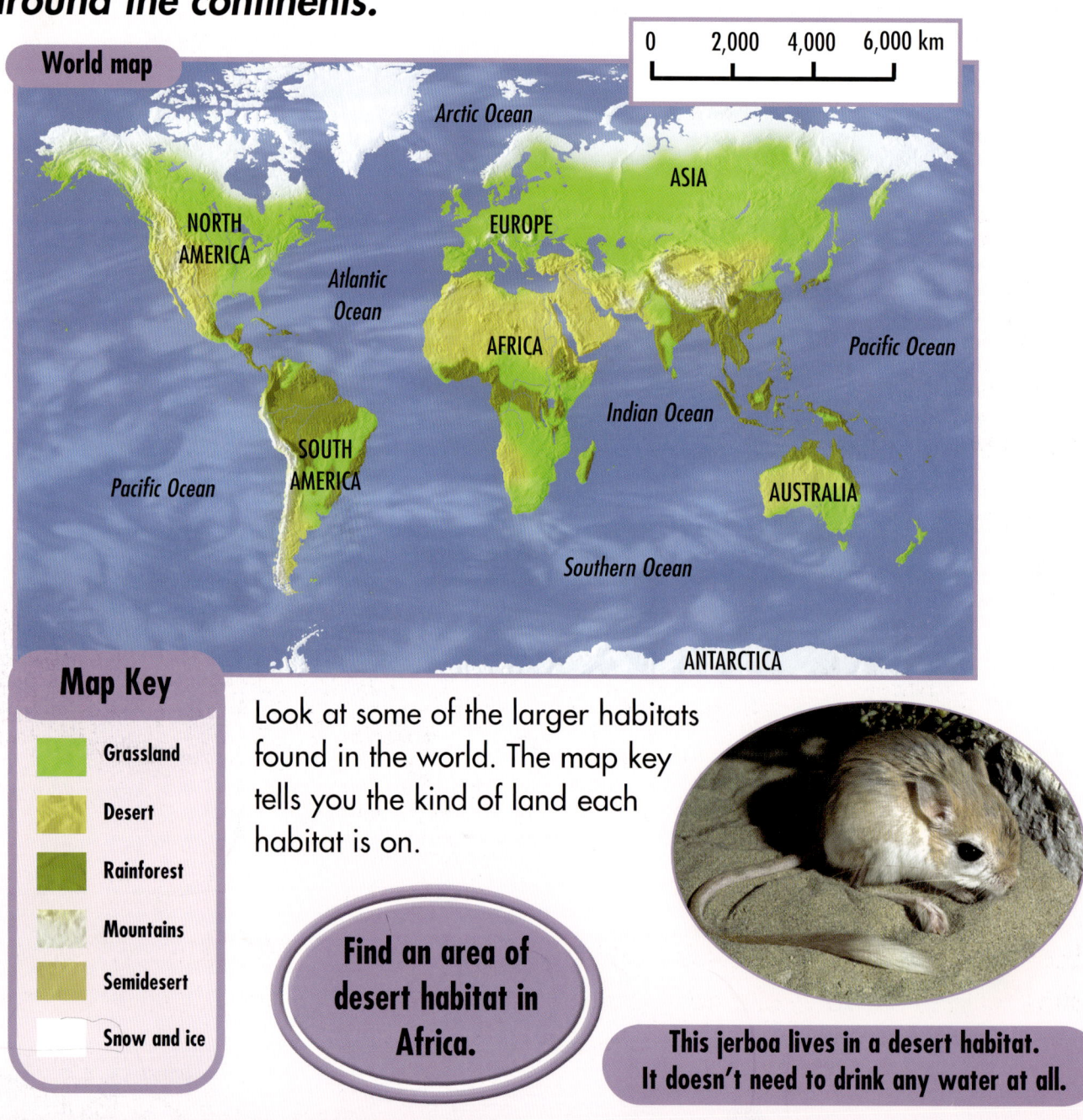

World map

0   2,000   4,000   6,000 km

Arctic Ocean
NORTH AMERICA
Atlantic Ocean
ASIA
EUROPE
AFRICA
Pacific Ocean
Indian Ocean
SOUTH AMERICA
Pacific Ocean
AUSTRALIA
Southern Ocean
ANTARCTICA

Map Key
- Grassland
- Desert
- Rainforest
- Mountains
- Semidesert
- Snow and ice

Look at some of the larger habitats found in the world. The map key tells you the kind of land each habitat is on.

Find an area of desert habitat in Africa.

This jerboa lives in a desert habitat. It doesn't need to drink any water at all.

Map of Europe

Most continents are divided into countries. Large oceans and seas surround the continents. The United Kingdom is on the continent of Europe.

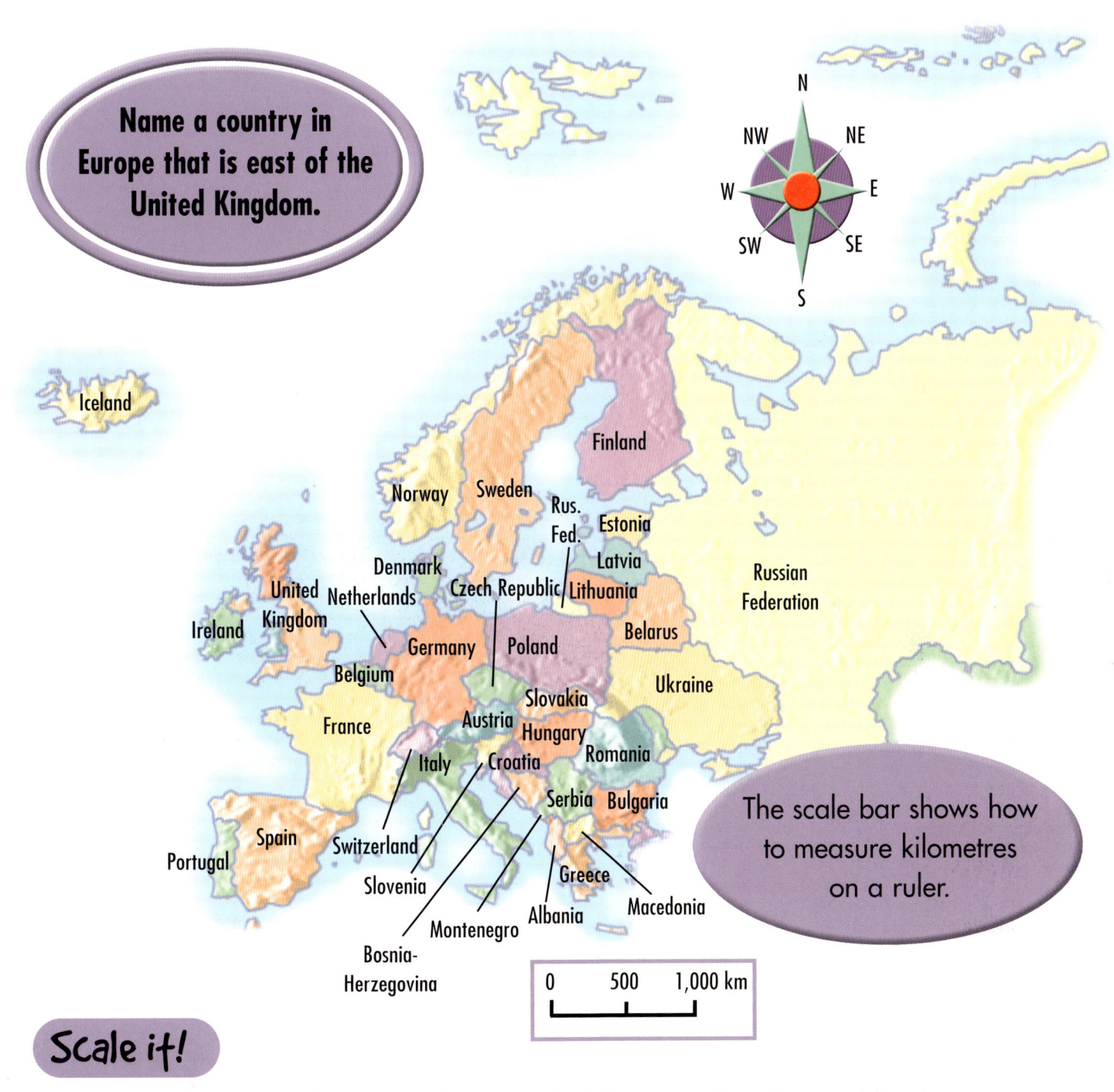

Name a country in Europe that is east of the United Kingdom.

Iceland
Norway Sweden
Finland
Rus. Fed. Estonia
Denmark Latvia
United Kingdom Netherlands Czech Republic Lithuania
Russian Federation
Ireland
Belarus
Germany Poland
Belgium
Ukraine
Slovakia
France Austria
Hungary
Italy Croatia Romania
Serbia Bulgaria
Spain Switzerland
Portugal Slovenia Greece
Montenegro Albania Macedonia
Bosnia-Herzegovina

0   500   1,000 km

The scale bar shows how to measure kilometres on a ruler.

N, NE, E, SE, S, SW, W, NW

Scale it!

Look at the two maps. They were drawn with different scales. The world map shows the entire world and has a smaller **scale**. The map of Europe shows one continent and has a larger scale. You can see details such as the countries' names and borders.

15

A map of habitats in Australia

Australia is a continent. It is also its very own country! Australia is very large and has many different habitats.

The colours on the map show the largest habitats in Australia. The map key tells you what the colours stand for.

Eastern Australia has lots of forest habitats. The koala lives there. It eats only Eucalyptus leaves from the forest.

Map Key

- Grassland
- Desert
- Forest
- Mountain
- Mangrove swamp
- Semidesert
- Reef
- River, lake or ocean

Much of Australia has desert and semidesert habitats. Often, the desert is called the outback.

Uluru is a huge rock formation in the outback of the region of Australia known as the Northern **Territory**. Its watering holes and rock caves attract many desert animals.

The red kangaroo is one of many animals that live in the desert.

The Great Barrier Reef

The Great Barrier Reef is an underwater habitat in Australia. Many fish and other sea creatures live among the coral reefs.

The hard coral reef is made from the skeletons of little sea animals. There are many types of coral. Some are flat. Some look like lace. Some even look like your brain!

Mapping a watering hole in Australia

A watering hole is a sunken area of land that fills with water. In Australia's outback, a watering hole can be a habitat for desert animals. They gather there to drink the water and cool off. A watering hole can be natural or man-made.

In Australia, natural watering holes like this one attract different desert animals.

The dingo, a type of wild Australian dog, can live in many different habitats.

Red kangaroos can go for a long time without water, by eating plants.

This man-made watering hole is part of a very large cattle ranch, also called a cattle station. It has a high rim around it that holds the water in place.

There is little rainfall in this habitat. The only plants are dry bushes. At this watering hole, there is also a small fenced area for rounding up, or mustering, the cattle.

Map Key

- Cattle
- Earth bank
- Fence
- Animal trail
- Water
- Dry earth
- Vegetation
- Trees

The map of this watering hole uses symbols to represent the different animals, objects, and **land features** around it. The map key helps you understand what the different symbols stand for.

More map information

This map uses colour to show temperature ranges around the world in the month of January. The map key colours show the highest and lowest temperatures in each range. What is the temperature range where you live?

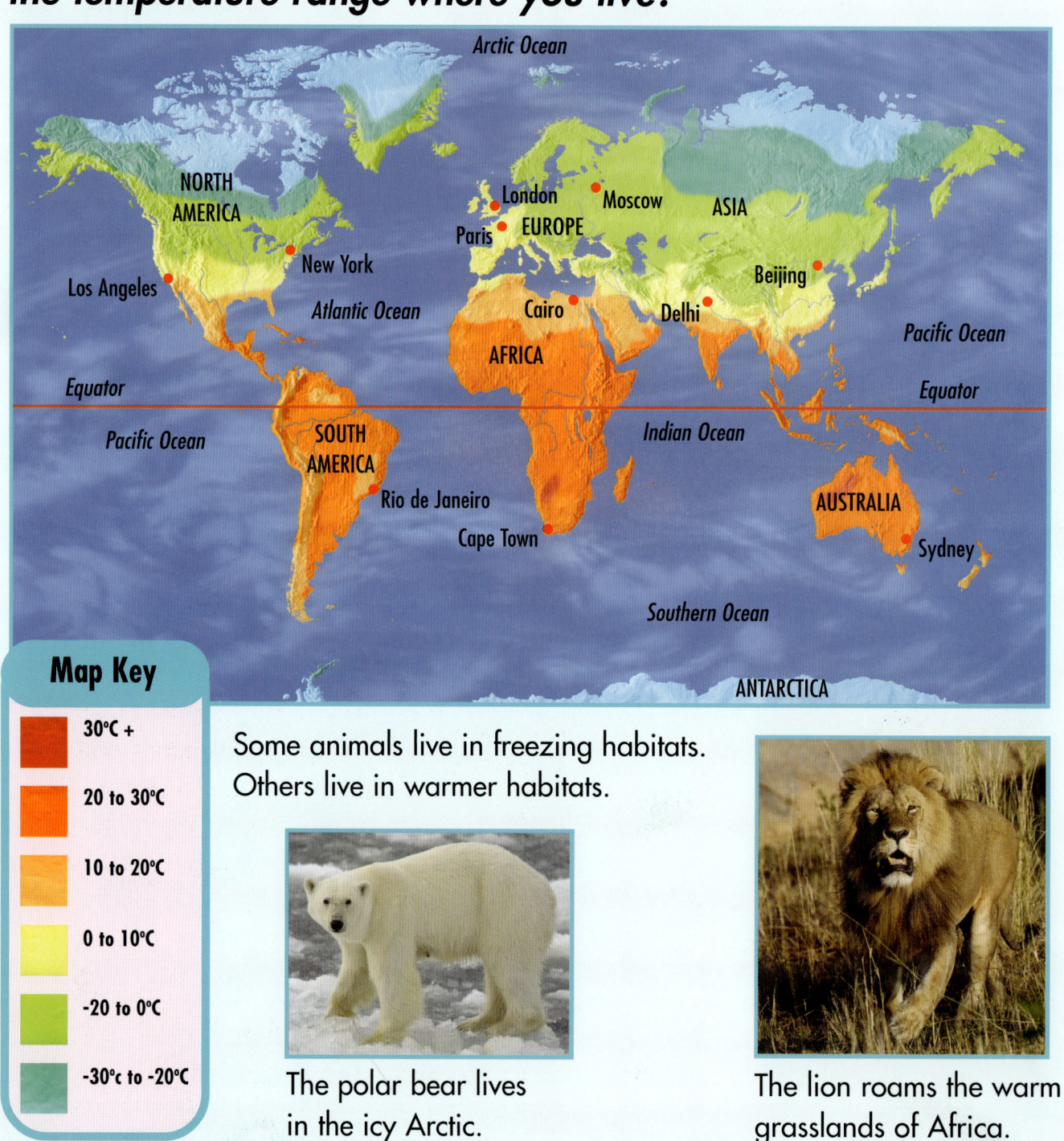

Map Key
- 30°C +
- 20 to 30°C
- 10 to 20°C
- 0 to 10°C
- -20 to 0°C
- -30°C to -20°C

Some animals live in freezing habitats. Others live in warmer habitats.

The polar bear lives in the icy Arctic.

The lion roams the warm grasslands of Africa.

Using a map grid

A **grid** is a mapping tool drawn over a map. It helps you find a specific place on the map. A grid is made of lines that form squares.

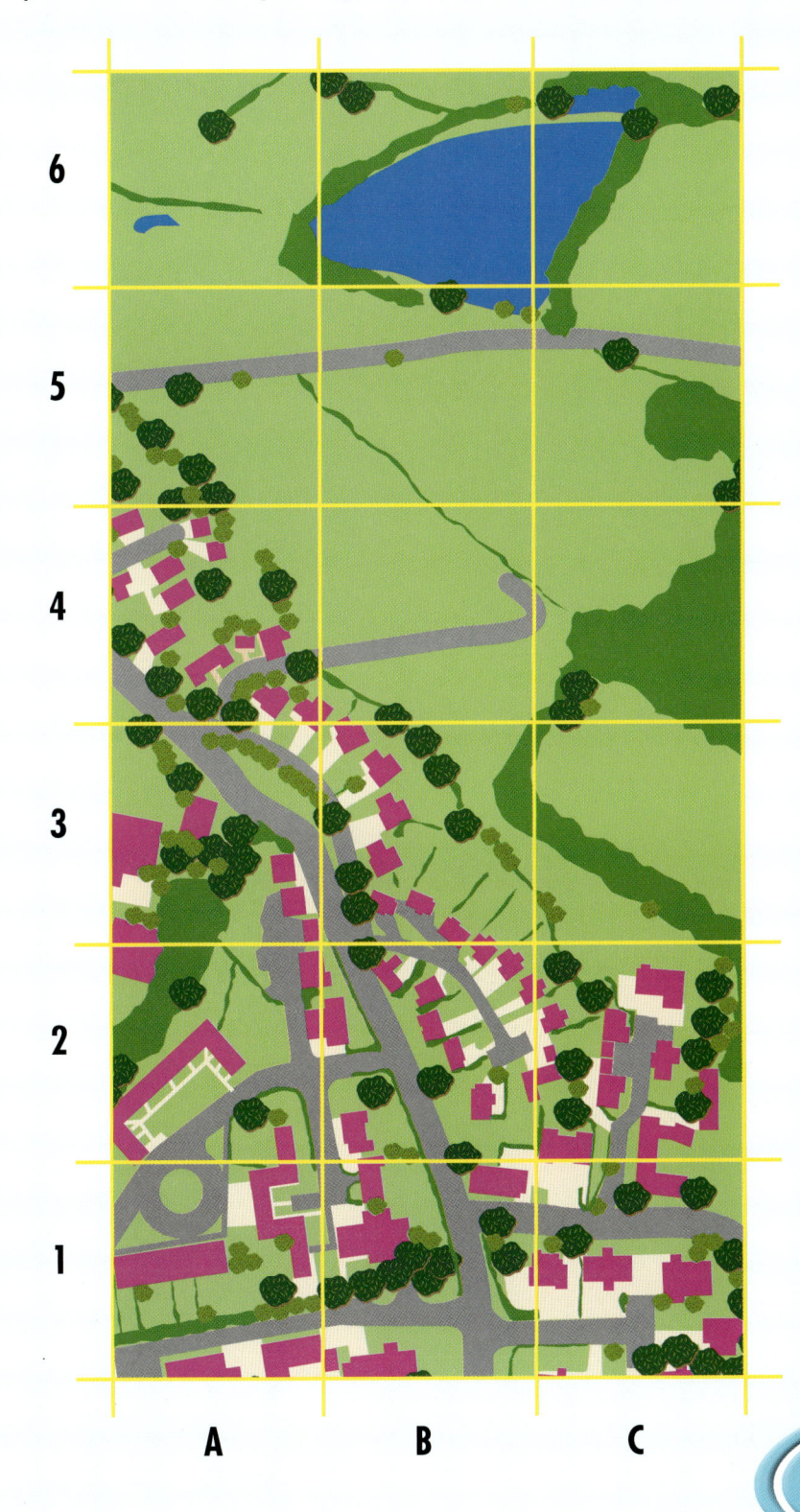

The squares on this map go left to right to make rows. Each row has a number. The squares also go from bottom to top to make columns.

Each column has a letter. Each square can be identified by both a letter and number. Together, the letter and number are called **coordinates**.

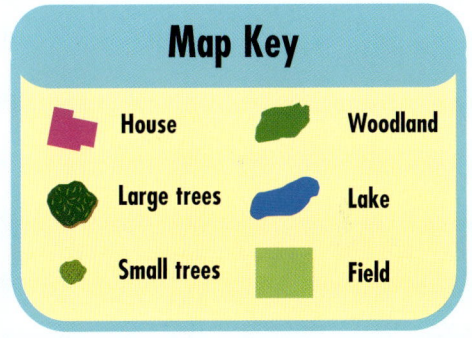

Map Key

- House
- Woodland
- Large trees
- Lake
- Small trees
- Field

To find the lake habitat, check the map key. Its coordinates are B6. Put your finger on B. Move your finger up column B until you find row 6. The lake is there!

Give the coordinates of the largest woodland area.

21

Drawing maps

Before you can draw a map, you must figure out the exact size and shape of the mapping area. This means figuring out how to measure large areas.

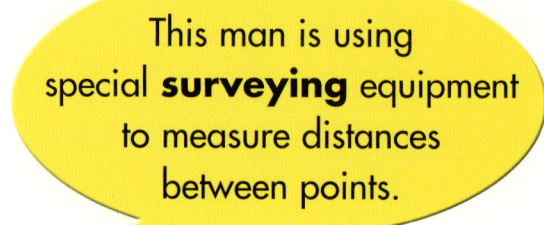

This man is using special **surveying** equipment to measure distances between points.

Mapmakers use their measurements to draw their maps. The maps on these pages show the attractions at an amusement park.

Scale: shrinking to fit

When mapmakers have gathered all their measurements, they must figure out how to fit them onto a piece of paper. So they shrink, or scale down, the real measurements to make a map.

0 — 15 metres

This small-scaled map shows a fairly large area. Many objects are visible, but they are quite small.

Different scales used to map the same area change what you see. Small-scale maps show large areas on a sheet of paper. Large-scale maps show smaller areas, but the objects look bigger and have more detail.

The map scale tells you how long a metre is on the map. This way you can figure out real distances on the map.

0 — 8 metres

This larger-scaled map shows a smaller area than the first map. The map scale also shows that each centimetre is equal to fewer metres. So you see fewer objects on this map, but you can see them in greater detail.

0 — 5 metres

This map has the largest scale. It shows an even smaller area. You see even fewer objects, but you can see them in even greater detail.

23

Hi-tech mapmaking

Many years ago, people used their travels to figure out the shape of the land. Today, mapmakers use new, **hi-tech equipment.**

Mapmakers can take many photographs of the ground from a plane.

This photograph shows the ground below as seen from the plane.

The pictures and measurements taken from the plane are sent to computers that draw a map.

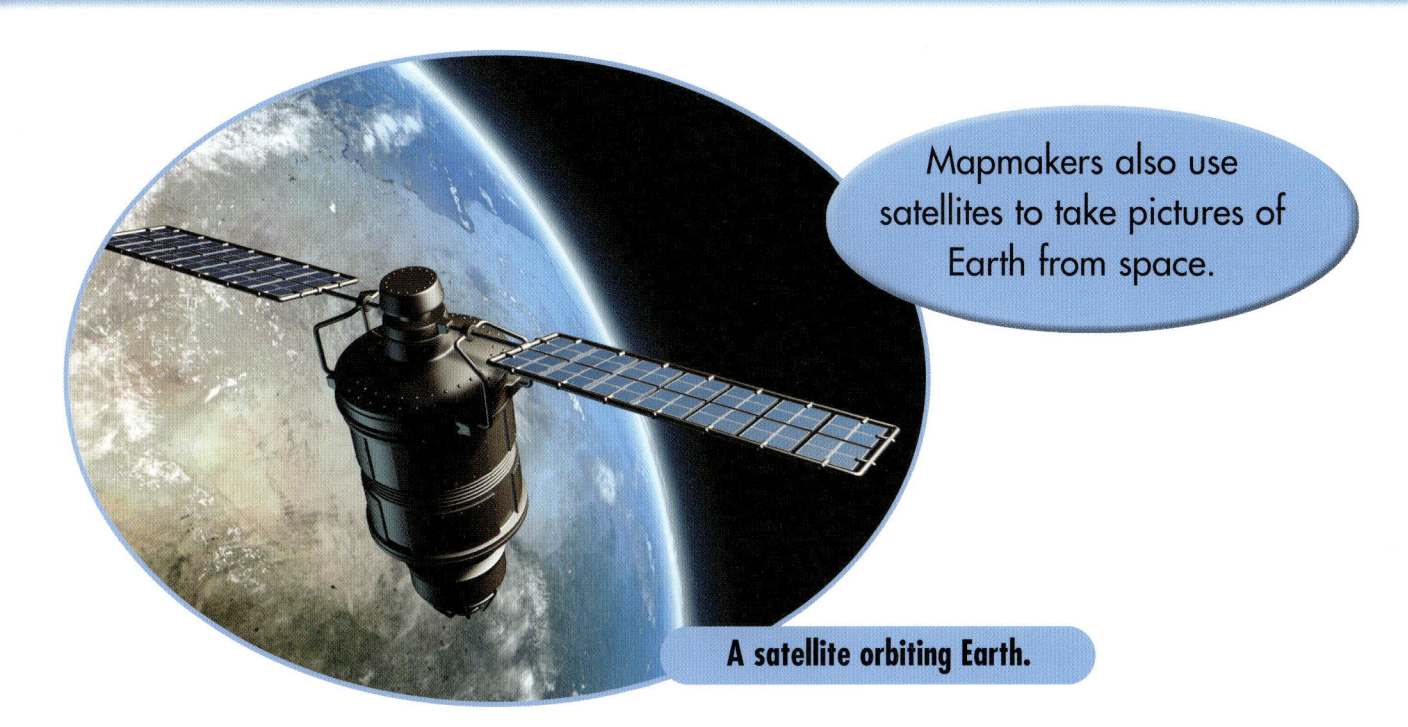

Mapmakers also use satellites to take pictures of Earth from space.

A satellite orbiting Earth.

The pictures taken by these **satellites** are beamed back to Earth. They are put together to make pictures of our planet, like the one shown here. These pictures can then be turned into maps.

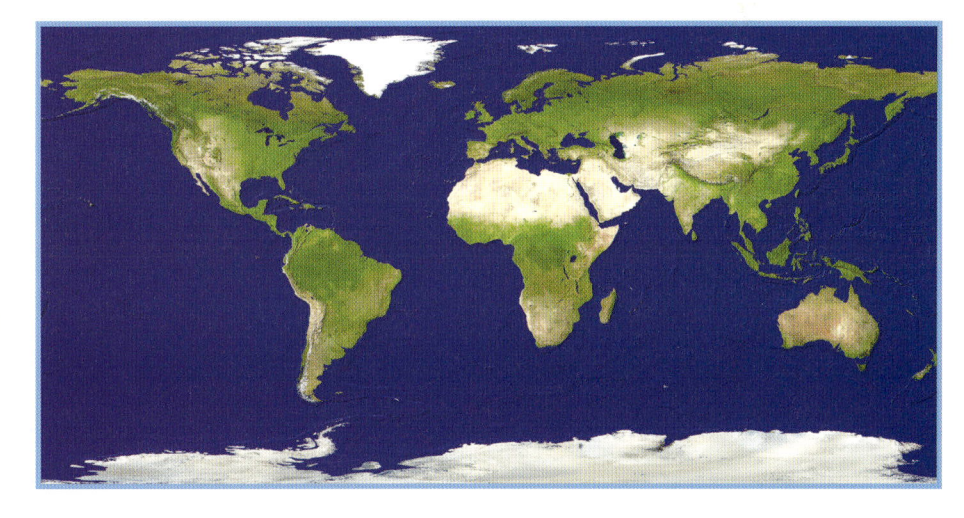

Ever-changing maps

Satellites can tell where your car is on the road. They can produce road maps that help you find your destination. These maps constantly change as you need them. The maps are called **GPS**, or Global Positioning System, maps.

A GPS map at work in a car.

25

Using a grid to map animal habitats in Australia

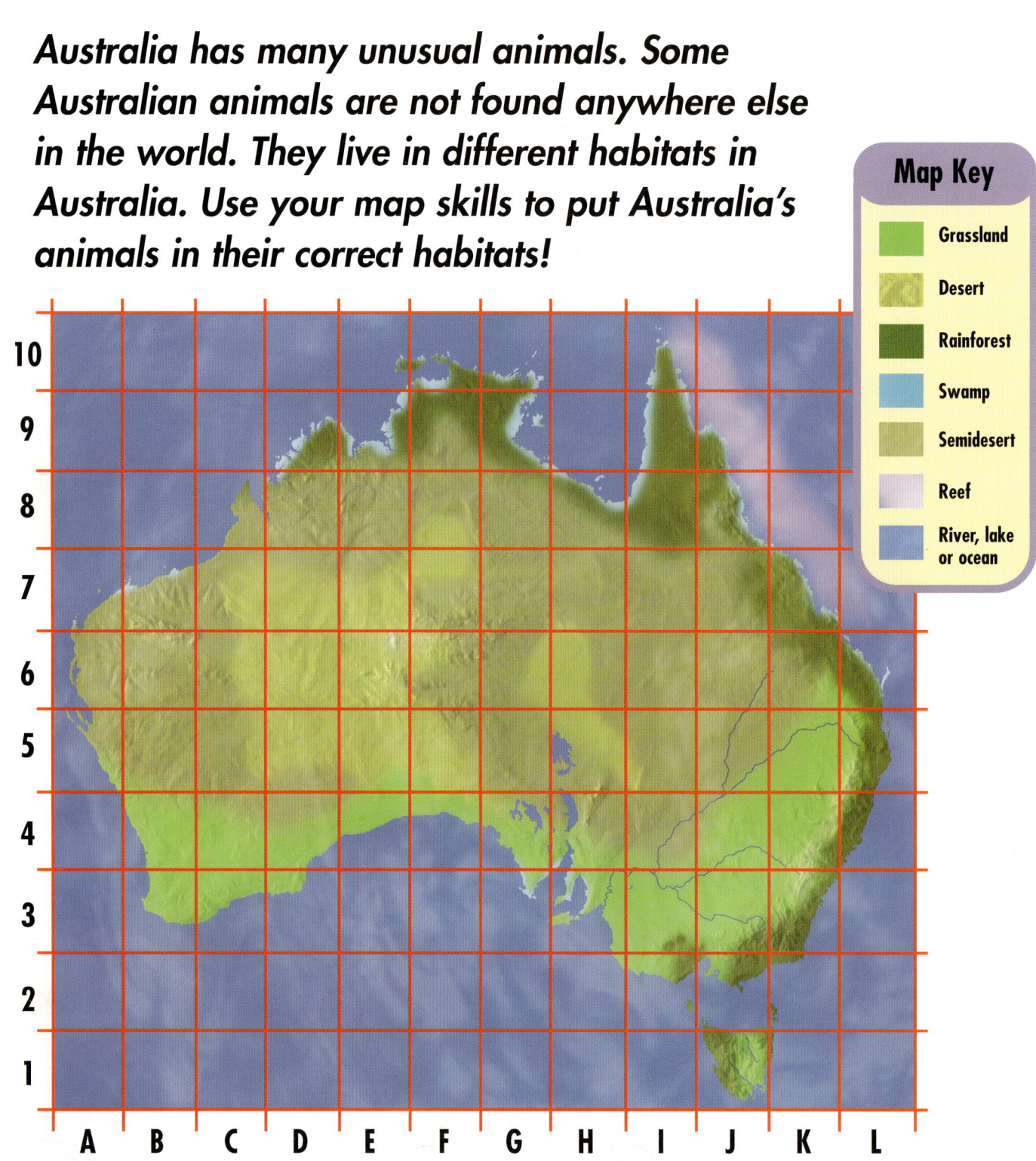

Australia has many unusual animals. Some Australian animals are not found anywhere else in the world. They live in different habitats in Australia. Use your map skills to put Australia's animals in their correct habitats!

Map Key
- Grassland
- Desert
- Rainforest
- Swamp
- Semidesert
- Reef
- River, lake or ocean

How to make a map of the animals of Australia

1. Copy the map of Australia on page 26 onto a blank sheet of paper. Colour your map to show the different habitats.

2. Now make a map key. Draw pictures on it of the animals you want to put on your map. Write down the names of the animals.

3. Use the grid references beneath the pictures to find each animal's coordinates on the map grid. (You can read about grids and coordinates on page 21.)

4. Follow the coordinates for each animal and draw the animals in their correct spots on the map.

5. Some of the coordinates contain more than one habitat. Which habitat seems best suited to each animal on your map?

Animal map key

- koala (L5)
- red kangaroo (I6)
- crocodile (G10)
- emu (D5)
- bottlenose dolphin (L4)
- thorny devil (D6)
- dugong (E10)
- tropical fish (K8)
- possum (J3)
- kookaburra (I8)
- dingo (H5)
- Tasmanian devil (J1)

Making a map of a habitat zoo

Have you ever been on a trip to the zoo? Why not create a map of your own zoo, filled with different kinds of habitats? Make sure you place your animals into their natural habitats.

What shape is your zoo? Round, rectangular, oval?

Does your zoo have a snack shop, public toilets, picnic tables, or drinking fountains?

William's Wonderful Zoo

Step 1

Draw the shape of your zoo on a piece of paper.

Step 2

Decide which habitats you want in your zoo and draw them in. Use colours and designs to represent the habitats. Map out a trail your friends can follow when visiting your zoo. Put in drinking fountains, rubbish bins, and other items you want to have in your zoo.

Step 3

Draw in the animals you have chosen to be in your zoo. Pick your favourite animals, and be sure to place them in their correct habitat!

Give your map a name.

Step 4

Make your map key using the symbols, colours, and designs on your map.

	Desert		Tigers		African elephants		Ticket office		Footpath
	Water		Anaconda snakes		Giraffes		Gift store		Snack shop
	Forest		Parrots		Meerkats		Toilets		Eating area
	Grassland		Monkeys		Camels		Rubbish bin		First aid
	Tropical forest		Polar bears		Marine turtles		Water fountain		Fence
	Arctic		Walrus		Tropical fish				Barrier

29

Glossary

Coordinates: a pair of numbers and letters used to locate a place on a map.

Depth: the length from the top of a space or an object to its bottom.

Government: a group of people who make the laws and rule in a country or area.

GPS (Global Positioning System): an instrument that tells a driver how to get to a place. As the car is moving, the instrument shows the driver directions on a screen.

Grid: a pattern of crisscrossed lines – usually horizontal and vertical – used as a way of finding locations on a map. Grids are often used to set up coordinates.

Habitats: areas or environments where plants or animals are most likely to be found. Most habitats are suited to certain kinds of life, such as fish (in a water habitat) or tropical plants (in a rainforest habitat).

Hi-tech (high-technology) equipment: computers and other electronic products made with the most modern scientific designs and materials.

Land features: natural areas found on Earth. Mountains, rivers, forests, and deserts are all land features.

Map key: the space on a map that shows the meaning of any pictures or colours on the map.

Moorland: a hilly wilderness habitat covered in grass and a plant called heather.

Satellites: objects launched into space by a rocket that circle and study Earth or other bodies in space. They then send information back to Earth.

Scale: the amount by which the measurement of an area is shrunk to fit on a map. The map scale is a drawing or symbol that tells how to measure distances on a map.

Surveying: using special tools to measure the area of land being mapped.

Symbols: pictures or drawings that stand for different things on a map.

Territory: area of land and water that belongs to a single country. Maps show borders of territories.

Three-dimensional (3-D): appearing as a solid thing that has length, width, and depth.

Two-dimensional (2-D): appearing as a flat shape with only length and width.

Wilderness: an area in which very few people live and that is mostly left in its natural state.

Index

A
Africa 14, 20
Amusement parks 22-23
Animals 5, 7, 8, 11, 13, 17, 18-19, 20, 26-27, 28-29
Arctic 20
Australia 14, 16-17, 18-19, 26-27

B
Birds 11

C
Cattle station 19
Cairngorms 13
Computers 24
Continents 14, 15
Coordinates 21, 27, 30
Coral reefs 17
Countries 15
Crops 7

D
Deer 13
Deserts 14, 17, 18-19
Dingo 18, 27
Drawing maps 22-23

E
Ecosystems 11
Eucalyptus 16
Europe 14, 15

F
Fish, tropical 27
Forests 7, 13, 16

G
Gardens 4, 8-9
Global Positioning System (GPS) 25, 30
Government 13, 30
Great Barrier Reef 16, 17
Grid 21, 26, 27, 30

H
Hi-tech mapmaking 24-25, 30

I
Insects 11

J
Jerboa 14

K
Kangaroo 17, 18, 27
Koala 16, 27

M
Map key 10, 12, 14, 16, 19, 20, 21, 27, 29, 31
Mapmaking 22-23, 24-25, 28-29
Microbes 11
Moorland 13

O
Outback 17, 18

P
Planes 24

R
Red deer 13
Red kangaroo 17, 18, 27
Roe deer 13

S
Satellites 25, 31
Scale 15, 22-23, 31
Surveying 22, 31

T
Temperature map 20
Trees 11

U
Uluru 17
United Kingdom 6, 12, 15

W
Watering holes 17, 18-19
Weather maps 6
Wilderness 13, 31
Woodland 11
World map 7, 20

Z
Zoo, habitat 28-29